Benvenuti
Anne-Marie Dalmais

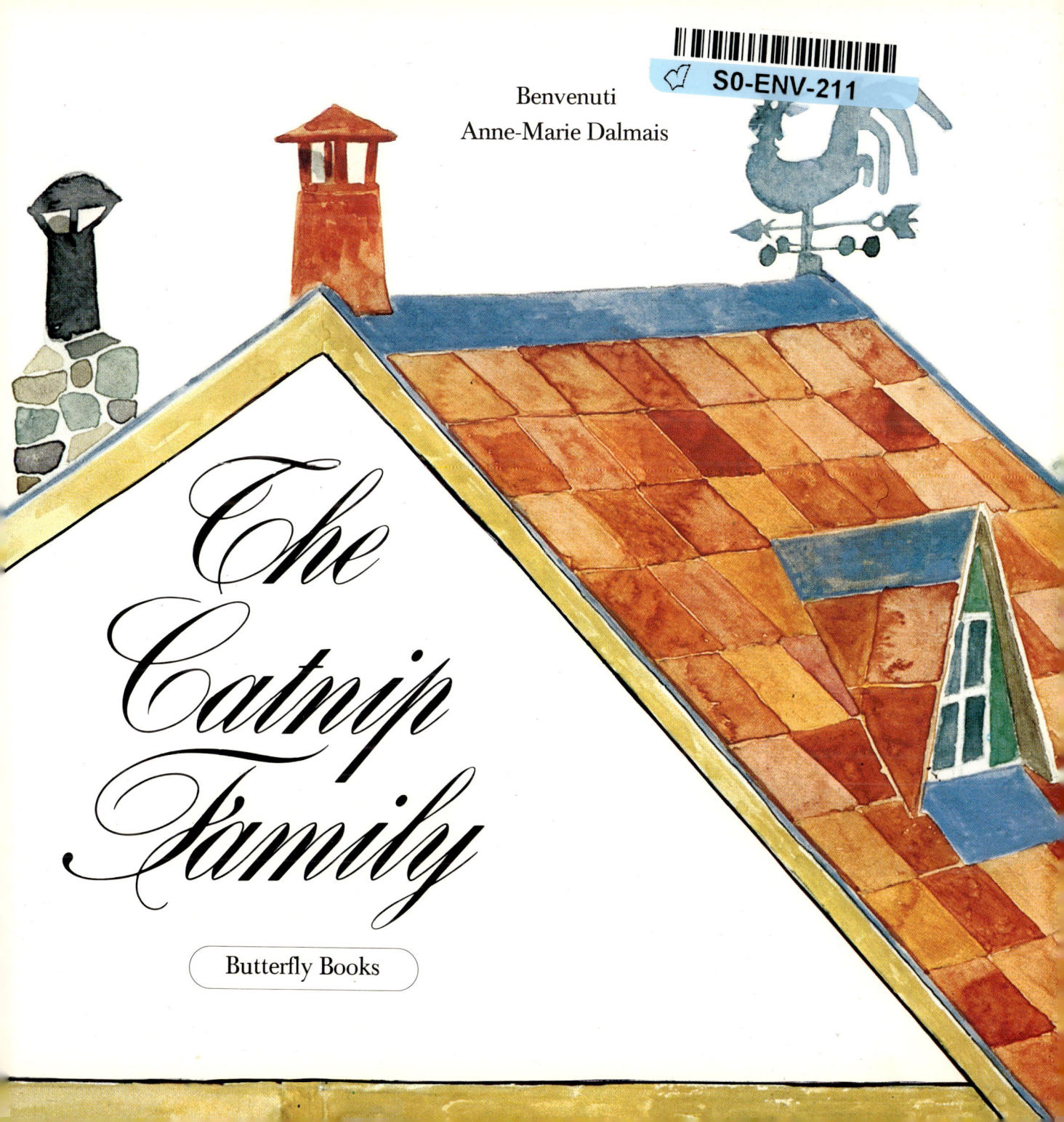

The Catnip Family

Butterfly Books

Do you know the Catnip family?
Let me warn you right away – they are all a little scatter-brained,
all a little nutty!
Let's stroll in through the garden. The flowers are really beautiful –
petunias, roses and tulips, daisies and wild iris. But look at the tools!
They've left them all over the place.

And the front door
of the house,
for some reason or other –
or perhaps no good
reason at all – is wide open...

coat rack

umbrellas

front door

door mat

We got here at just the right time! Sweet Mrs Catnip is about to lose her mind. She was having a chat with her neighbor Felina, there in the armchair, when...

a penetrating odor of burnt blueberries made her rush to her kitchen. Heavens, what a disaster! Intent on her conversation, Mrs Catnip had completely forgot the pie she had put in the oven for dinner!

sink

stove

tablecloth

tiles

curtain
toy chest
pillow
eiderdown
bed
Caramel
Clementine

There was a disaster upstairs, too,
but the overflowing bathtub just brought
smiles of surprise and delight
to the two Catnip children.

Caramel and his sister Clementine
had simply forgot that they were
running a bath. And it must have been
their model train's fault...
it was running perfectly!

As for Mr Catnip, he was not to be disturbed. In his shirt sleeves and keeping a careful eye on his watch, he hurriedly changed one of the tires on his car, having sworn to beat his record time of five minutes, fifty-five and one-fifth seconds...

house

road

pedal

I almost forgot to tell you that our friends
the Catnip family just loved the out-of-doors.

fence

field

Usually, when they decided to have a picnic,
they would leave their beautiful red car at home
in the garage and pedal away on bicycles.

Each had his own talent and technique: Caramel went straight for the fish, while Clementine would try to lure frogs with a piece of red rag.

can of worms

river

float

frog

fish

water-lily

Caramel

bucket

bank

butterfly

Clementine

basket

bicycle

flowers

fish-hooks

Mr. Catnip

tandem

sun hat

picnic basket

tablecloth

plate

bottle

Mrs. Catnip

Mr Catnip considered himself a champion fisherman, but Mrs Catnip, as you may well understand, had a slightly different opinion...
But despite such snags and upsets, the least we can do is wish the Catnip family a "Happy Picnic"!

This charming book also comes in a poster version, ready to brighten a child's wall. Your bookseller has it as well as others of the series.

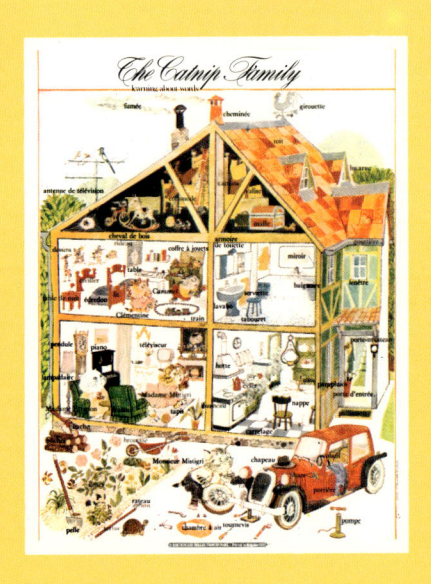

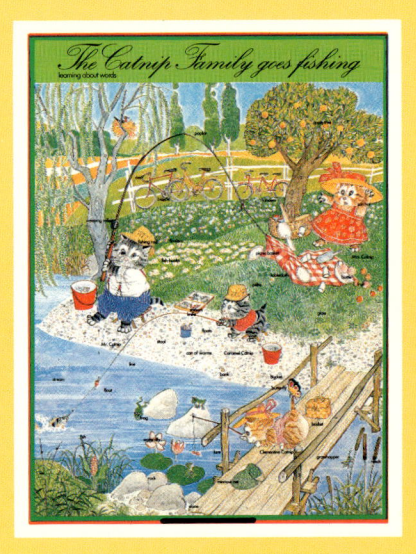

illustration
Benvenuti
text
Anne-Marie Dalmais
adaptation
Mel Wallace
design
Michel Cartacheff

Butterfly Books

TWO CONTINENTS PUBLISHING GROUP
30 East 42 Street, New York, New York 10017